AF573789

Possible sources of authority

It was Richard Hooker, one of the greatest of English theologians, who long ago drew attention to the three possible sources of authority in our religion; the Christian Bible, the Christian Church and the Christian Reason. These three possibilities have not been extended in the three centuries since his death, and we today must make up our minds what order of priority we shall assign to them.

It is plain that of the three great movements in Christendom, the 'Catholics' (including of course the Roman Catholics) have tended to emphasize the authority of the Church, orthodox Protestants the authority of the Bible, while the Liberal and Modernist movements have championed the authority of the Reason and Conscience.

It is equally plain that any extreme view which assigns all authority to one of these claimants, *while totally discounting the others*, leads at once to disastrous results: witness the intellectual shackles which fetter the Roman Catholic world, where Church authority is stressed to the exclusion of private judgment; witness the appalling subjectivism to which the modernism of the 1920s led, impatient as it was both of Church tradition and biblical testimony; and witness the endless fragmentation of the Protestant sects, where men have professed sole allegiance to one and the same Bible, but have neglected the exegetical tradition of the Church.

Bible, Church, Reason, all are necessary. They are complementary, and not contradictory sources of authority. Most people agree in theory that this is so; the difficulty comes in practice, when one or other of these three seems to be at variance. What is to be our final court of appeal?

The 'Catholic' View

To the Roman Catholic, the Church, inspired by the Holy Spirit, is the supreme authority in faith and morals. 'What does the Church teach?' is the question he asks himself. He does not ask the prior question 'On what grounds does the Church teach it?' because that would be to question the authority he has decided is supreme.

Thus, to take an example in the realm of belief, it is

incumbent on the Roman Catholic to believe that the Virgin Mary ascended up bodily into heaven, since this dogma was defined in 1950. He *has* to believe this, because the Church through its teaching organ, the Pope, has declared it to be so, although there is not a shred of early evidence to support it.

Similarly, in the realm of behaviour, a Roman Catholic who marries a Christian of another denomination *must* be married in a Roman church by a Roman priest, or else be accused of living in sin, and be excommunicated as a result. Although there is nothing in Scripture or Reason to demand this, the faithful Roman Catholic must obey his supreme religious authority, the Church. Naturally, the Church recognizes the authority of Holy Scripture, but only as interpreted by herself. In short, on this view the Bible is authoritative because it is part of Church tradition, which both interprets and supplements it.

Now the position of the Roman Catholic is at least clear and logical. But the same cannot be said for those 'Catholics' who are not Roman. It is all very well to say that the Church is the arbiter of faith and morals, the ultimate authority in religion. But what is the Church? What is its teaching organ? Where may we find its decrees? And which of its traditions are reliable? Roman Catholics know the answer to these questions—at any rate since the Vatican Council of 1870 decided that the Pope was infallible when speaking *ex cathedra!* But what would an Anglo-Catholic or an Eastern Orthodox churchman say? This recourse to the teaching of the Church is hardly as attractive as it appears at first sight, nor is 'the Church' as clear and united in its proclamations as one might hope from 'the final authority under God'.

The 'Liberal' View

Then there is what we might call the Liberal view. The word is in rather bad odour today, and there are many varieties of view among Liberals, but it would be fair to say that all agree in making the human reason, conscience, or religious insight (illuminated, of course by the Holy Spirit), the nearest to a final authority under Christ that we possess.

On this view, the Bible is inspired, because it is the work of religious genius. The word 'inspired' is used in much the same sense as when it is applied to Shakespeare's plays or Handel's music. Some Liberals try to make room for the idea of revelation; God revealed Himself through the gropings of man towards Him; and this, in their view, is the subject matter of the Bible. Others have allowed no room for the supernatural activity of God in history, but maintain, in the words of one writer (*Scottish Journal of Theology*, May, 1958) that 'both in form and content the Bible entirely shares the laws that govern secular literature'.

Such a view, of course, cannot begin to come to terms with what the Bible claims for itself. And in reaction from this negative attitude, there has recently been a renewed emphasis on the Bible as being the Word of God alongside the words of men. Some would say that the Bible *is* not the Word of God, but *contains* it. The difficulty here is that of discernment. How are we to tell the Word of God from the rest? How are we to sift the wheat from the chaff? If the answer is 'Accept the assured results of modern criticism', that does not get us very much further. Quite apart from the fact that this is merely to replace the Pope on his throne by the Professor of Biblical Studies in his chair, such a procedure leads to complete uncertainty.

Few things, it would seem, are less assured than the 'assured' results of modern criticism. Critical orthodoxy for almost a hundred years has assumed the essential correctness of the Graf-Wellhausen documentary hypothesis about the Pentateuch, the priority of Mark among the gospels, the existence of a lost document known as 'Q' which recorded the sayings of Jesus, and the lateness and historical unreliability of St John's Gospel. But in the last few years all these 'assured' results have been heavily assailed by capable scholars!

It would seem then, that this 'Liberal' method of approaching the Scripture is no less free from grave objection than the 'Catholic' view considered earlier. Though the scholars have to a large extent abandoned it, the minds of many people both within and without the Church are still affected by it. They feel that 'even the parsons who ought to believe the Bible don't, so why should we?' In this way, an authority which has claimed to be an alternative to biblical authority has turned out in practice to be no authority at all.

We cannot pick and choose with documents which claim to embody the truth of God. If their claim is accepted, then they should be trusted and obeyed. If not, then the sooner they are exposed the better. And this last is exactly what 2000 years of rigid scrutiny and criticism of the Bible has been unable to do. To quote some words of Dr Ramsey, the previous Archbishop of Canterbury, 'The methods and results of modern critical study may be shewn to compel no denial of the authority of the Bible, but rather to assist our understanding of the ways in which it is true, inspired, and the Word of God in revelation' (Art. 'Authority of the Bible' in *Peake's Commentary*, 2nd edn. 1962).

The 'Traditional' View

In view of the unsatisfactory nature of the alternatives, it is hardly surprising that the Christian Church has been remarkably at one about the prime place of Scripture. The teaching of the Church which is indwelt by the Holy Spirit is indeed most important. The enlightenment of the Christian mind and conscience by the Holy Spirit is no less essential. But it is to the Scriptures inspired by the Spirit that Christians have habitually turned as the nearest to an ultimate authority that mortal men can find.

Indeed, until the rise of the Liberal movement a little more than a century ago, the Church throughout the world, the Church throughout the ages, had spoken with one voice in assigning to the Bible the supreme authority in all matters of Christian belief and Christian life.

In the Lambeth Report of 1958 this traditional position was reaffirmed by the Bishops of the Anglican Communion. 'The Church is not *over* the Holy Scriptures, but *under* them, in the sense that the process of canonization was not one whereby the Church conferred authority on the books, but one whereby the Church acknowledged them to possess authority. And why? The books were recognized as giving the witness of the Apostles to the life, teaching, death and resurrection of the Lord, and the interpretation by the Apostles of these events. To that apostolic authority the Church must ever bow' (*Report on the Holy Bible* 2.5). The Report also stressed that we ought not to pick from the biblical message those elements which happen to be congenial, while rejecting what we do not like (*op. cit.* 2.13). And in so stressing the supreme authority of Scripture over both Church and Reason, our Bishops have merely been following the lead of the Church from the beginning.

The statements of the Churches

Roman and reformed Churches

Typical of the attitude of the early Church is this affirmation of the great scholar Origen, in the third century: 'The sacred books were not the work of men; they were written by the inspiration of the Holy Spirit, at the will of the Father of all, through Jesus Christ' (*de Principiis* 4.9).

The official teaching of the Church of Rome takes the same attitude: 'The Synod, following the example of the orthodox fathers, receives and venerates all the books of the Old and New Testament, seeing that one God is the author of both' (*Session* 4 *of the Council of Trent*).

The Lutheran Formula of Concord says: 'The Holy Scriptures alone remain the only judge, rule and standard according to which all dogmas shall be discerned and judged.'

The Westminster Confession, the official statement of Presbyterian belief, states: 'All the books of the Old and New Testament are given by inspiration of God, to be the rule of faith and life'. Examples could be multiplied. And, of course, the emphasis of the Church of England is identical, both in the Prayer Book and Ordinal.

The Church of England

Practically every word of the Services is drawn from the Bible; large amounts of Scripture are included as lessons, psalms and canticles in Morning and Evening Prayer and the Holy Communion. And the sixth Article of Religion expressly states: 'Holy Scripture containeth all things necessary to salvation: so that whatsoever is not read therein, nor may be proved thereby, is not to be required of any man, that it should be believed as an article of the Faith'.

So strongly does the Church of England feel about this, that she emphasizes it again and again in the ordination of her priests.

In the first place, they are to study the Scriptures, 'And seeing that you cannot by any other means compass the doing of so weighty a work, pertaining to the salvation of man, but with doctrine and exhortation taken out of the holy Scriptures, and with a life agreeable to the same; consider how studious ye ought to be in reading and learning the Scriptures . . . and for this self-same cause ye ought to forsake and set aside (as much as you may) all worldly cares and studies . . . that, by daily reading and weighing of the Scriptures, ye may wax riper and stronger in your ministry.'

In the second place they are to believe and teach the Scriptures. 'Are you persuaded,' asks the Bishop of the candidate, 'that the holy Scriptures contain sufficiently all doctrine required of necessity for eternal salvation through faith in Jesus Christ? And are you determined out of the said Scriptures to instruct the people committed to your charge, and to teach nothing (as required of necessity to eternal salvation) but that which you shall be persuaded may be concluded and proved by the Scripture?'

In the third place, they are to tolerate no unscriptural teaching. 'Will you be ready, with all faithful diligence, to banish and drive away all erroneous and strange doctrines contrary to God's Word . . .?' asks the Bishop. 'I will, the Lord being my helper,' replies the candidate for the priesthood.

And as a final reminder of the source of all the Church's teaching, the Bishop gives the ordinand a Bible, with the words, 'Take thou authority to preach the Word of God'. This emblem of the work of the Ministry is all the more striking when we remember that before the Reformation each priest was given not a Bible but a chalice.

It should be plain from all this, that recourse to the Bible as the supreme authority in the Christian religion is no mere idiosyncrasy of obscurantists and fundamentalists. It is the avowed intention of the Universal Church, and not least of the Church of England, however little it may be carried out in practice.

Christ and the Old Testament Scriptures

The reason for this unanimity is not far to seek. It stems from the attitude of our Lord Himself towards the Scriptures.

Two attitudes to the Old Testament in the time of Christ

There were those in the days of His flesh, who set the voice of the living community alongside the historic word of God as enshrined in the Old Testament. The Scribes and Pharisees held to an oral tradition which was professedly a 'fence for the Law', but in practice took the place of the Law of Moses and even reversed its decisions. When the two were in competition, the tradition was often preferred, as the saying of Rabbi Johanan frankly admits, 'Words of Soferim (i.e., tradition) are more beloved than words of Torah (i.e., the Law of Moses)'.

The Rabbinic writings altered the written word of God in two ways. They made additions to its enactments, giving details, for instance, of thirty-nine types of work which they forbade on the Sabbath! This accounts for Jesus' words of rebuke in Luke 11.46, 'You [lawyers] load men with burdens hard to bear, and you yourself do not touch the burdens with one of your fingers.'

They also subtracted from the regulations of the Old Testament, as in the celebrated case of the Corban (Mark 7.9-11). The details of this legal wangle are a little obscure but it is abundantly clear that the Scribes and Pharisees were setting their traditions over against what Moses taught about the necessity for honouring parents.

This Pharisaic view of authority, which set tradition alongside Scripture, was the ancient counterpart of what we have called the Catholic view. It is noteworthy, then, that this position drew from Jesus' lips some of the fiercest words of condemnation that He ever used. See Luke 11. 37-52, Matthew 23.16-24, and especially Mark 7.1-13. He could not bear to have the word of God made void by the traditions of men (Mark 7.13).

The Liberal view of Scriptural authority also had its exponents in ancient Judaism. The Sadducees accepted only the Pentateuch among the sacred writings, and in the well-known story of the woman with seven successive husbands (Matthew 22.23-33) Jesus not only confuted their unscriptural denial of the resurrection out of the very books which they *did* accept, but he blamed them for their culpable ignorance of the Scriptures and the power of God.

As we shall see in a moment, Jesus' attitude to the Old Testament was in striking contrast to that of both the Pharisees and the Sadducees. Despite the attractive alternatives of Tradition and Reason, it was to the Old Testament that He turned as His authority in all disputed points of belief and behaviour. This attitude of reverence for and obedience to the Bible was not induced by the absence of any other prevailing attitude in His own day; rather, He rejected both the Catholic and the Liberal answers to the problem of authority, and took His stand upon the written Word of God. Let us then examine Jesus' attitude to the Old Testament.

Christ's own attitude to the Old Testament

1. In the first place, *He studied it carefully, and framed His life and teaching in accordance with it.* In the story of the Temptation, three times He met the Devil's suggestions with quotations from the book of Deuteronomy (Matthew 4.4, 7, 10[1]). This suggests not only that He saw the Scriptures as a powerful weapon against spiritual adversaries (see Ephesians 6.17), but also that He made a habit

[1] from Deuteronomy 8.3; 6.16; 6.13.

of studying the Bible carefully and committed key verses to memory.

Not only this incident, but His constant apt quotation of the Old Testament shows His deep and reverent study. We find that He began His Ministry in accordance with the Scriptures (Luke 4.16, 17[1]). It was in the Old Testament Scriptures that He saw His role as anointed Messianic Son of God (Mark 8.29; 14.61[2]). It was there that He saw His destiny as the Suffering Servant of the Lord (Mark 10.45[3]) and as the Son of Man (Mark 14.62.[4]). It was in accordance with the Old Testament predictions that He healed (Matthew 11.5; Matthew 8.16f[5]) and taught in parables (Matthew 13.35[6]). He suffered in accordance with those same scriptures. 'This scripture must be fulfilled in me, "And he was reckoned with transgressors"; for what is written about me has its fulfilment' (Luke 22.37). He allowed Himself to be hounded to death, because 'everything that is written of the Son of Man by the prophets will be accomplished' (Luke 18.31; see also Mark 14.21). His resurrection, too, was foreshadowed in the Old Testament.[7] We find Him explaining: 'Thus it is written, that the Christ should suffer and on the third day rise from the dead' (Luke 24.46). Indeed, this is exactly what He taught His closest followers about the resurrection long beforehand, little though they might understand it (Mark 10.33; Matthew 12.40; Mark 9.9; John 16.22; Luke 24.6-8).

Not only the life of Jesus, but His teaching also is rooted in obedience to, and fulfilment of, the Old Testament. In the Sermon on the Mount, for instance, the Beatitudes owe much to the Psalms and Isaiah; and even those injunctions in other parts of the Sermon which appear to contradict the Old Testament actually carry its teaching to a deeper level. For example, when Jesus says (Matthew 5.27), 'You have heard that it was said, "You shall not commit adultery". But I say to you that every one who looks at a woman lustfully has already committed adultery with her

[1] see Isaiah 61.1ff.
[2] see Psalm 2.7; 110.1.
[3] see Isaiah 53.12; cf. Matthew 26.54.
[4] see Daniel 7.13,14.
[5] see Isaiah 35.5; 61.1; 53.4.
[6] see Psalm 78.2.
[7] Isaiah 52.13; 53.10; Psalm 110.1; Psalm 16.8-11.

in his heart,' He is not contradicting but intensifying the standard set forth in the Seventh Commandment (Exodus 20.14).

Or take the idea of the New Covenant, which He consecrated with His own blood on the Cross. 'This cup is the new covenant in my blood,' He said (1 Corinthians 11.25).[1] His words refer back to Exodus 24.8, 'Behold the blood of the covenant which the Lord has made with you' and Jeremiah 31.31, 'Behold, the days are coming, says the Lord, when I will make a new covenant with the house of Israel. . . .' Here again Jesus was fulfilling an Old Testament motif.

Think, too, of just one aspect of His teaching about His death. He said that He would give His life a ransom for many (Mark 10.45). The Old Testament had made it plain that through sin a man's life is forfeit—'the soul that sins shall die' (Ezekiel 18.4). Now, 'no man can ransom his brother, or give to God the price of his life' (Psalm 49.7mg). What man cannot do for another, nor indeed, for himself (Mark 8.37), Jesus undertook to do for all men, to give His life a ransom for the many, as the prophet foretold.[2]

One could show how Jesus' teaching about the 'little flock' (Luke 12.32) and the good shepherd (John 10) are based on Ezekiel 37, or how favourite metaphors like the vine and the fig tree derive from the Old Testament.[3] One could point out how, when asked which was the most important of God's laws, His reply was Jewish orthodoxy itself, being derived from Deuteronomy 6.4 and Leviticus 19.18, 'You shall love the Lord your God with all your heart' and 'You shall love your neighbour as yourself' (Mark 12.30f). It is clear beyond all doubt that Jesus soaked Himself in the Old Testament Scriptures, studied them, and framed both His life and teaching in accordance with them.

2. A second characteristic of Jesus' attitude to the Old Testament is that *He regarded it as inspired by God.* And by 'inspired' He certainly did not mean merely that it was wonderful literature, or inspiring to read. He meant that

[1] cf. Mark 14.24 and parallels.
[2] Isaiah 53.5,6,8,12.
[3] eg Mark 12.1 from Isaiah 5.1ff., and Luke 13.6 from Habakkuk 3.17.

behind the human author God Himself was the Author of the Scriptures. How else can we understand Mark 12.36, 'David himself, inspired by the Holy Spirit, declared . . .', quoting Psalm 110? The same point is underlined in Mark 7.13, where He declared that the Pharisees were making the word, not primarily of Moses or the prophets, but the word of *God* void through their tradition. It is plain that when He speaks of the 'desolating sacrilege set up where it ought not to be' (Mark 13.14) he regards the book of Daniel as divinely inspired prophecy of the days which were soon to come. When He is upbraiding the Sadducees for their hardness of heart and incredulity (Matthew 22.31), He says, 'As for the resurrection of the dead, have you not read what was said to you by *God*, . . .' (quoting Exodus 3.6).

In an illuminating passage in John 5.36-47, particularly significant because of the solemnity of the subject under discussion (the eternal destiny of the hearers), Jesus refers to the Scriptures as the God-given witness to Himself, of greater importance than either John the Baptist's testimony to Him, or the miracles that He Himself did. The Pharisees search the Scriptures, because they hope to find eternal life through them; but they will not come to Jesus, to whom the Scriptures point (vv. 39, 40). They make Moses and his writings the object of their hope; but Moses wrote of Jesus (v. 46), whom they have rejected. Both Jesus and Moses' writings come from God. They hang together as complementary parts of God's self-revelation. But when men will not believe Moses' words, it is hardly surprising that they will not accept those of Jesus (v. 47). Here Jesus coordinates His own words and authoritative commission from God with that of Moses, and explicitly sets His seal on the divine inspiration of the Old Testament Scriptures. One could multiply examples of this sort, such as John 17.12, 'None of them is lost but the son of perdition; that the scripture might be fulfilled'; or Matthew 26.54, 'But how then should the scriptures be fulfilled, that it must be so?' Quite plainly Jesus accepts the prophetic scriptures as divinely inspired.

But perhaps the crowning example of His attitude is to be found in Matthew 19.4, 5. It is all the more impressive because it is so natural. Jesus is quoting the words of Genesis 2.24, in itself a comment passed by the author of Genesis, and He ascribes them to God Himself. 'Have you not read that *he who made them . . . said*, "For this reason a man shall leave his father and mother and be joined to his wife"?' Clearly, Jesus regarded this statement of the author of Genesis as nothing less than spoken by God Himself, even though the Genesis account does not directly attribute it to the Almighty. A word of Scripture was a word of God.

3. The third notable thing about Jesus' attitude to the Old Testament, is that *He regarded it as absolutely authoritative*, both for Himself and others. We have seen some of the evidence for this above, with His emphasis that the Scriptures *must* be fulfilled.[1] In Matthew 5.17, 18, the very passage where He goes on to interpret the Old Testament and enlarge on its teaching, He says, 'Think not that I am come to destroy the law, or the prophets: I am not come to destroy, but to fulfil. For verily I say unto you, Till heaven and earth pass, one jot or one tittle shall in no wise pass from the law, till all be fulfilled' (AV). This is a truly remarkable expression of biblical authority, for the 'jot' is the *yôdh*, the smallest letter in the Hebrew alphabet, and the 'tittle' the little stroke which differentiates certain Hebrew letters!

In discussion of controversial doctrinal issues with the theologians of the day, Jesus had constant recourse to Scripture as His authority. Was it the question of the resurrection from the dead? Then to Scripture they must go, and the Sadducees' error lay in their failure to do so (Mark 12.24). Was it a question of what might or might not be done on the sabbath? To Scripture He would go, and base His argument and His practice on biblical precedent (Matthew 12.3, 5). We have already seen how ethical problems, such as divorce, were settled by Jesus in the same way, by reference to Scripture. We have seen how He treated it as the final authority for His understanding of His own mission and destiny.

Indeed, in one place, He makes the whole force of His argument depend upon a single biblical word (John 10.34),

[1] Matthew 26.53-54; Luke 18.31; 22.37 etc.

'Jesus answered them, "Is it not written in your law, 'I said, you are gods'? If he called them gods to whom the word of God came (and Scripture cannot be broken) do you say of him whom the Father consecrated and sent into the world, "You are blaspheming," because I said, "I am the Son of God"?' One might think this is a singularly indiscreet *obiter dictum* of the psalmist's (Psalm 82.6), and very liable to misinterpretation as polytheism, but Jesus maintains that even here the Scripture cannot be broken. 'The judges of Israel had been entitled, in a sense, to be so called, because they represented however imperfectly, the divine will in so far as they were called upon to administer God's word' is how Professor R. V. G. Tasker explains the original reference.[1] The point that concerns us at present, however, is that Jesus and the Jews to whom He is speaking are agreed in their doctrine of Scripture. It is supremely authoritative, because it is inspired by God Himself. It would make no difference if, as some scholars maintain, Jesus' argument is specifically *ad hominem* here. Indeed, His words may have more than a touch of irony about them, as He refuses to allow His opponents to escape from the consequences of their own holy books. For Psalm 82.7 continues, 'Nevertheless, you shall die like men!' In any case the fact remains that the Jews and Jesus are at one on this issue; *the Scriptures cannot be broken.*

Throughout all the strata of evidence preserved to us of the teaching of Jesus, He treats the argument from Scripture as having clinching force. When He says, 'It is written,' that is final.

This subordination both in doctrine and practice to the Scriptures is a very remarkable feature in One who claimed such paramount authority for Himself and His teaching. He caused great astonishment in the Palestine of His day because 'He taught them as one who had authority, and not as the scribes' (Mark 1.22). The people wondered, 'How is it that this man has learning, when he has never studied?' (John 7.15; *cf* Mark 6.2-4). The answer, of

[1] *St John's Gospel*, p. 134. Similarly Prof. R. H. Lightfoot writes (*St John's Gospel*, p. 209), 'If, then, according to the Scriptures, divinity in some sense may be or has been ascribed to recipients of "the word of God", who, however, showed themselves unworthy of the trust reposed in them, what justification have the Jews for bringing the charge of blasphemy against Him, the Word made flesh, who is now doing the works of His Father?'

course, was given in His reply, 'My teaching is not mine, but his who sent me' (John 7.16). His teaching came with all the direct authority of God Himself: 'What I say, therefore, I say as the Father has bidden me' (John 12.50). But although He claimed to possess the ultimate authority of God, so much so that the eternal destiny of His hearers depended on whether, once they had heard His words, they kept them (Matthew 7.24ff); yet never once do we find Him opposing His own authority to that of the Old Testament. Never once does He qualify the current belief in its supreme authority for faith and conduct.[1]

This, then, was our Lord's attitude to the ancient Scriptures. He reverently studied the Old Testament; He regarded it as inspired by God; and He treated it as divinely authoritative. This attitude is to be found in all the four gospels. It is to be found in Mark, the 'Q' material, and the special contribution made by Matthew and Luke independently. It is to be found most emphatically in the Fourth Gospel. It is to be found perpetuated by the apostles, His closest associates, in their preaching of the Gospel.[2] Every strand of evidence about Jesus of Nazareth tells the same story. If this does not represent the real attitude of Jesus, we must account the whole New Testament record as hopelessly unreliable, and resign ourselves to knowing nothing at all about Him with any degree of certainty.

What is more, this attitude of Jesus to the Old Testament remained unchanged throughout His life. We find it in His temptation. We find it in the first sermon at Nazareth. We find it throughout His ministry. We find it at the crisis of His life in the arrest, agony, and upon the cross itself. After the resurrection it was still the same. There is no suspicion of any change in His view of scriptural authority as His mission developed.

Kenosis and Accommodation

The force of this evidence is widely recognized among scholars, but attempts are still made to evade it in two ways, the kenosis theory and the accommodation theory.

[1] For apparent exceptions, see below under 'Accommodation Theory' pp. 19f.

[2] eg Acts 2.29-31; 3.18,21,24; 4.24,25.

The Kenosis Theory maintains that the process of the incarnation made it inevitable that the Son partook of the errors and prejudices of His time, among them the current view of scriptural authority. The passage which gave rise to this theory, Philippians 2.7, says that Jesus *ekenosen* (emptied) Himself. In the context, the reference would seem to be not to the incarnation at all, but to the atonement; not to a supposed laying aside of His divine attributes, but to the 'pouring out his soul to death', as in the best texts of Isaiah 53.12. However, this apart, there are serious theological objections to be brought against this 19th century theory of kenosis. Of course our Lord's knowledge was limited to some extent by the incarnation; so was His omnipresence and omnipotence, or His would not have been a genuine human life.

The Gospel records tell us specifically of one thing Jesus did not know, the time of His return in glory (Mark 13.32). But limited knowledge is not the same thing as error; and to say that Jesus was in error at any point is a serious admission for anyone who holds that the claims of Christ to be the Son of God were vindicated at the resurrection (Romans 1.4). He Himself claimed that all He taught was divine truth;[1] and if He was mistaken about the very nature of authority in religion, why do we still call Him Lord? If He was wrong about the inspired nature of the Old Testament, on which He based His whole conception of His mission, then He could well have been wrong about everything. It is impossible to reject Christ's teaching about the authority of the Old Testament without abandoning belief in His own authority and the uniqueness of His person and His work.

Furthermore, it is significant that He taught the same high doctrine of Scripture after His resurrection, when, presumably, the alleged 'kenotic' limitations on His omniscience imposed by the incarnation had been removed. He still believed in the prophetic inspiration of the Scriptures; He still believed in their relevance to His person and mission; He still recognized their binding authority.[2]

[1] Mark 13.31,32; John 12.48.
[2] Luke 24.25-27,44-46.

It would seem, then, that the kenosis theory will not do. If it proves anything, it proves too much. The inspired character of the Old Testament is integral to the life, work and authority of Jesus Christ. As John Stott puts it: 'It is very dangerous to begin with the presupposition "to err is human", and then to add "therefore, to be human, Jesus must have erred". Could we not equally well argue that "to sin is human, and therefore Jesus must have sinned"?. . . . Though both sin and error are part of our fallen human nature, they are no necessary part of the perfect human nature which God made and Christ assumed. The evidence of Scripture is that the man Christ Jesus, through the perfect surrender of His mind to the revelation of God, was inerrant, and through the perfect surrender of His will to the will of God, was sinless.'[1]

An alternative to the kenosis theory is the *Theory of Accommodation*. Upon this view we are to suppose that Jesus deliberately refrained from enlightening His hearers about the untrustworthy nature of the Old Testament. Although in His divine wisdom He did not share their regard for its inspiration and authority, nevertheless He 'accommodated' Himself to the prejudices and ignorance of His contemporaries. And the proof that He did so is shown by His radical attitude to the Old Testament in Matthew 5.17-48, by His 'liberal' attitude to the Sabbath, and by His sweeping rejection of the Mosaic teaching on divorce. Such is the theory.

The accommodation theory, however (quite apart from the moral questions it raises as to His intellectual integrity) fails to explain why Jesus adopted exactly the same attitude when teaching His intimate disciples as He did when preaching to the crowds. Surely this is remarkable procedure in one supposed to be consciously accommodating Himself to popular prejudice?

Furthermore, we know that Jesus was not unduly worried about upsetting dearly cherished errors! It was Jesus who in no small degree precipitated His country's disastrous clash with Rome. It was Jesus who so exposed the traditionalism and corruption of the religious leaders that they hounded Him to death. Why, then, was He

[1] J. R. W. Stott, *Fundamentalism and Evangelism* (Crusade, 1956), p. 17.

willing to compromise the truth by 'accommodating' Himself to prevailing views of Scripture if He thought them erroneous?

Thirdly, this view fails to take account of the tremendous moral earnestness of passages like Luke 16.29-31 and Mark 7.6, 13, where His complete acceptance of the Old Testament and its authority is most clearly marked.

As for these three places where a more radical attitude to the Old Testament is supposed to have been adopted by Jesus, let us examine them briefly. They are concerned with the Sermon on the mount, the Sabbath, and Divorce.

1. THE SERMON ON THE MOUNT. (Matthew 5.17-48 in particular.) Quite clearly Jesus is contrasting the Old Testament teaching, at any rate as expounded by the Pharisees, with His own words. But vv. 17, 18 warn us against the facile assumption that He is seeking to contradict the Old Testament. How could He possibly say, 'Verily I say unto you, Till heaven and earth pass, one jot or one tittle shall in no wise pass from the law,' if He were at the same time launching an attack on its authority? What Jesus is in fact attacking here, is not the Old Testament itself, but the rabbinic misuse of it. Jesus Himself enters into the spirit of the Old Testament law, and develops it further. For example, in its context (see Exodus 21.24), 'an eye for an eye and a tooth for a tooth' (quoted in Matthew 5.38) was not designed to justify revenge but to *limit* it. Only fair retribution could be required by an injured party who was out for blood! And Jesus takes that same principle further, to an extent that would have been quite impossible in the wild, rough days of the Exodus, by prohibiting revenge altogether: 'Resist not evil . . . turn the other cheek'. Revolutionary teaching, true; but in line with the original intention of Old Testament command.

If proof were needed that it is the traditional interpretations of the scribes which Jesus is attacking and not the Scripture itself, v. 43 provides it. Here the Old Testament says, 'You shall love your neighbour' (Leviticus 19.18), but it certainly *does not* go on to say 'and hate your enemy'. That addition was made by the scribes, no doubt in consideration of the frailty of human nature! But it effectively undermined the whole purpose of the divine command, which was to encourage love of others, not to show whom one could legitimately hate. And so when Jesus says, 'I say to you, Love your enemies,' He is merely expanding the ideal of the Old Testament, carrying on, as it were, where it left off. He is most certainly not undermining its command, but rather attacking the limiting clause of 'and hate your enemy', attached to it by the theologians of the day.

2. THE SABBATH. Here again, it looks at first sight as though Jesus is guilty of a very casual approach to the sabbath day. But what, in fact, did He do on the sabbath which caused such resentment among the religious leaders? He taught with power, He healed sicknesses, apparently both psychological and physical.[1] And on a sabbath walk in the countryside He raised no objection when His disciples plucked corn as they passed and rubbed it in their hands to eat it (Mark 2.23-28). It is easy to miss the point here. What the disciples were doing was not dishonest; it was perfectly permissible to pluck corn as one walked through a neighbour's field (Deuteronomy 23.25). What the Pharisees fastened on to was the rubbing of the ears of corn to extract the wheat. This was threshing! And threshing was forbidden by the scribes as a sabbath day employment. Similarly in the case of the blind man of John 9, it was because Jesus had made clay by spitting into the dust, and had anointed the man's eyes with it, that the Pharisees were so incensed (v. 16). By making clay in this way He had broken one of their myriad laws which they erected as a 'fence' for the sabbath, but which, in fact, spoiled its whole purpose. For God had given man the sabbath as a day for worship, for service and for rest. It was to be a delight (Isaiah 58.13), but the theologians had turned it into a day of misery for the ordinary people. It was against this that Jesus was protesting in His unusual behaviour on the sabbath. He was getting back to the Old Testament ideal which had been lost sight of through the petty restrictions of the scribes and Pharisees.

3. DIVORCE. Twice in St Matthew's gospel Jesus deals with divorce, and appears to lay down a more rigid

[1] Mark 1.21-34; 3.1-6, etc.

standard even than Moses.[1] He is clearly opposed to the 'bill of divorce' that Moses gave. Surely, then, He must be setting up His authority against Moses? In chapter 5 Jesus does indeed cite Deuteronomy 24.1, 'Whoever divorces his wife, let him give her a certificate of divorce'. But He does not say that Moses *approved* of divorce. Moses did not institute or sanction divorce, but brought in this regulation in order to *limit* it and bring some justice into a situation over which he had no control. As far as it went, a 'bill of divorce' was some slight alleviation of distress. It afforded the woman protection from the arbitrary command to 'clear out at once' which a bad-tempered or drunken husband might utter on a sudden impulse, only later to claim the woman back. It was at least a step in the right direction; and, of course, Jesus' teaching of the wrongness of divorce altogether is a great advance on it.

But in chapter 19 the Pharisees are foolish enough to claim Mosaic authority for divorce as such (and not merely for the 'bill of divorce' prescribed in Deuteronomy 24.1ff). At once Jesus tells them (19.8) that Moses certainly did not authorize divorce. Why, in the first Book of Moses, God's ideal for man and woman stands revealed. A man shall 'leave his father and mother, and be joined to his wife, and the two shall become one' (19.5 from Genesis 2.24). Moses' enactment about the 'bill of divorce' is not meant to annul that original plan of God, but rather to restrict by human regulation the hardness of the man's heart who refuses to abide by God's plan for marriage.

It would appear, then, that these three instances where Jesus seems to set His authority against the Old Testament will not begin to bear the weight placed upon them by the advocates of the accommodation theory. So far from holding a low estimate of Scripture and accommodating Himself to the erroneous high view of it current in His day, it is clear that Jesus saw His own teaching as the fulfilment of the divinely inspired and supremely authoritative Scriptures of the Old Testament. Neither the accommodation nor the kenosis theory satisfactorily evades the cumulative force of all the evidence we have considered.

[1]Matthew 5.31; 19.7,8.

In every strand of the tradition about Jesus, the same view of Scripture emerges. He treated it as the inspired message of God to men, the final court of appeal in all matters of faith and conduct. And if this was the attitude of the Master, should it not be that of the disciple who seeks to be loyal to Him?

The New Testament

But there is more to come. Granted that we should accept the Old Testament as inspired by God and authoritative, because Jesus Himself did so, then what are we to make of the New Testament? Did Jesus envisage any such extension of Holy Scripture? Is it, too, inspired? Does it, too, command our obedience?

The purpose of Jesus

The Old Testament, as we have seen, is authoritative for the Christian because Christ has set His seal upon it. The New Testament is authoritative because it contains the testimony of the apostles to this same Jesus. It was the deepest conviction of the early Christians that Jesus was the crown of God's self-revelation to men, the Word of God not merely contained in a book, but actually made flesh, as St John puts it (1.14). Jesus Christ is the supreme revelation of the Father, and all revelation before Him was fragmentary and incomplete. 'In many and various ways God spoke of old to our fathers by the prophets; but in these last days he has spoken to us by a Son' (Hebrews 1.1). For this reason we should not be surprised to find that the disciples failed to understand, in the days of His flesh, a good deal of His significance.[1] Always in the past, God had revealed Himself by His mighty deeds in history, and by the record and interpretation of them in the words of Scripture. Event and interpretation went hand in hand. And so it would have seemed natural enough· to His

[1] eg Mark 8.17-21; Luke 9.45.

disciples when Jesus said to them, 'I have yet many things to say to you, but you cannot bear them now. When the Spirit of truth comes, he will guide you into all the truth . . . He will glorify me, for he will take what is mine and declare it to you' (John 16.12-14). The Holy Spirit would equip them to interpret the greatest event in the entire history of God's revealing and redemptive work—the person and significance of Jesus Christ.

It is important to notice that it was to the *apostles* that this important task was committed. They were to bear witness to Jesus, because they had been with Him from the beginning, and they were to have the help of the Holy Spirit who would constantly bear witness to Jesus (John 15.26), remind them of what He had spoken (John 14.26), and guide them into further appreciation of Jesus, who is the truth of God (John 16.13). What we have in our New Testament, then, is the apostolic testimony to the words and deeds of Jesus, and the meaning of His life, death and resurrection, as the apostles were led to understand it through the Holy Spirit. That is why the apostles are sometimes called in the New Testament 'the foundation of the Church' (Ephesians 2.20; Revelation 21.14). They are the bottom storey in the building of the Church; they were in immediate contact with Jesus on earth. They are the divinely-equipped recorders and interpreters of His person and achievement.

It will help us to appreciate the unique function of the apostles, if we recall that they were the commissioned messengers of Jesus Himself. To the Jew, the commissioned messenger, or *shaliach*, always carried the authority of his master—an authority, incidentally, which he could not pass on to anyone else. 'He that is sent is as him that sends him,' said the rabbis. And this seems to be exactly what our Lord means in verses such as Matthew 10.40, 'He who receives you receives me,' and John 20.21, 'As the Father has sent me, even so I send you'. Christ was sending the apostles out with full powers to represent Himself.

We see this happening in the Ministry itself, as a pointer to what was to come later on after the resurrection. In Matthew 10 Jesus sends out the twelve apostles, clothed with His authority (v. 1). Their message is His message (v. 7), to preach the nearness of the kingdom of heaven. Their function is His function, as the prophets had foretold (Isaiah 35.5f; 61.1f) to heal the sick, cleanse the lepers, raise the dead, cast out devils (v. 8). It is precisely the same programme that He Himself fulfils in the next chapter, 'the blind receive their sight and the lame walk, lepers are cleansed and the deaf hear, and the dead are raised up . . ." (11.5). In other words, the apostles are so united with the work of Jesus that they are uniquely able to continue it after His ascension, and to interpret it with authority for later generations: 'He that is sent is as him that sends him'. They are the commissioned delegates of their ascended Lord, and as such their authority is His own. Thus in the great commission of Matthew 28.18, 19, Jesus can say, 'All authority in heaven and on earth has been given to *me*. *Go* therefore. . . .' The apostles are clothed with the authority of Christ Himself. Such was the purpose of Jesus.

The claim of the apostles

Not only have we good reason to think that this was the plan of our Lord, but it was also the emphatic claim of the apostles themselves.

St Peter, for one, has no hesitation in claiming that the same Holy Spirit of God which inspired the prophets is at work in the apostles of the Christian era (1 Peter 1.11, 12). In his second epistle he puts 'the predictions of the holy prophets' and 'the commandment of the Lord and Saviour through your apostles' on the same level (3.2), and includes Paul's writings among 'scripture' (3.16). Though at first sight this looks strange, it is consistent. For Peter has already said (1.21) that what characterizes Scripture is that holy men of God spoke as they were moved by the Holy Spirit. If the same Holy Spirit is leading the apostles into all the truth, why should not their words and writings have the same binding authority as the Old Testament and the words of Jesus, whose mouthpiece they were (1 Peter 4.11)?

It was not only St Peter who claimed for the apostolic teaching this position of equality with the authoritative writings of the Old Testament. St John does just the same.

The claim is present in 1 John 1.1-5, and is strongly emphasized in 2 John 10, 'If anyone comes to you and does not bring this doctrine, do not receive him into the house or give him any greeting'. Adherence to the teaching of the apostles is made the condition of Christian fellowship. Similarly, throughout the book of Revelation the same high claim is made, culminating in 22.18, 19, the passage that claims finality for the apostolic message enshrined in the book.

Needless to say, Paul claims the same unique authority for the apostolic message, whether written or oral. In Galatians 1.6-12 he invokes a solemn curse on anyone who departs from the gospel which he had been preaching; for he knew himself to be the apostle of Jesus Christ, personally commissioned by the ascended Lord to be His chosen representative among the Gentiles. In 1 Thessalonians 2.13 he gives thanks that when the Thessalonians received the gospel message, they received it, not as the mere word of men, but, as it is in truth, the word of God. In his second letter to this Church he says that rejection of his teaching must involve excommunication.[1] In 1 Corinthians 2.16 he claims the very mind of Christ, and insists that not only his doctrine, but the words in which it is couched, are inspired by the Holy Spirit (2.13). In 1 Corinthians 7, where many people think that he is at pains to distinguish between the importance of his teaching and that of Jesus,[2] he exclaims, 'This is my rule in all the churches!' (7.17). He is the apostle of Jesus Christ, and therefore his authority is that of his Lord. That is why he can say, 'If any one thinks that he is a prophet, or spiritual, he should acknowledge that what I am writing to you is a command of the Lord. If any one does not recognize this, *he is not recognized!*' (1 Corinthians 14.37, 38).

This is how the apostles viewed their authority, and this is how they exercised it. In the Acts of the Apostles we

[1] 2 Thessalonians 3.14; *cf.* 1 Timothy 6.3,5.

[2] In 1 Corinthians 7.10, Paul quotes a saying of Jesus on divorce, and quite naturally exclaims, 'To the married I give charge, not I but the Lord. . . .' In verse 12 he has no recorded saying of Jesus to cite, and therefore says, 'I say to the rest, not the Lord. . . .' He is not distinguishing between degrees of authority (verse 17 makes that clear) but is simply making it plain when he is, and when he is not quoting the words of Jesus.

find them building up the infant church, working miracles just as their Master had done (Acts 5.12), exercising stringent discipline (5.1-11), issuing directives (16.4), organizing the internal administration of the church (6.1-4), and preaching with God-given boldness and effect (2. 41-43). The fellowship and authorized teaching of the church is their fellowship and teaching (2.42). They are the Lord's representatives, both for building up the Church (2 Corinthians 10.8) and for judging it (2 Corinthians 13.1, 2). An apostle, 'in the name of the Lord Jesus,' even delivers a hardened and impenitent Church member 'to Satan' (1 Corinthians 5.3-5). They were in every sense the Master's men, clothed with His authority because chosen by Him as His representatives.

The testimony of the early Church

If this position of supreme authority in the Church was claimed by the apostles themselves, and envisaged and authorized by Jesus Himself, we must now ask whether the early Church endorsed their claim. Did they regard the apostolic teaching as their standard both in belief and behaviour?

The answer is perfectly plain. They did. Not only is this clearly presupposed by the gnostic appeal to esoteric apostolic tradition, but the orthodox Christian writers of the sub-apostolic age explicitly say so. Clement of Rome, for instance, writing about AD 95, says, 'Christ is from God and the apostles from Christ' (ch. 42), and in a later chapter is careful to distinguish the *apostles* Peter and Paul from Apollos, 'a man approved in their sight' (ch. 47). Ignatius, who was martyred c. AD 115 was the first monarchical bishop that we know of, and by no means inclined to underrate the importance of his office! He thinks that the bishop is the very image of God, and yet he writes to the Romans, 'I do not command you, like Peter and Paul did. They were apostles' (*Romans* 4). And in a famous passage to the Philadelphians (ch. 5) he puts the prophets, the apostles and the gospels on the same authoritative level. Again, Polycarp, writing c. AD 116, says, 'Let us so serve Jesus with all reverence and fear as He has Himself given us commandment, as did the apostles who preached the gospel to us, and the prophets who proclaimed beforehand the coming of the Lord' (*Polycarp* 6). And so one could go on.

The men of the sub-apostolic age were acutely aware of the distinction between the apostolic age and their own, and they emphasized it by constant reference to the writings of the New Testament. They freely applied the formula 'It says' or 'The Scripture says' to the New Testament as well as to the Old Testament writings. This is surprising only to those who do not take seriously the New Testament doctrine of the unique function of the apostles. Indeed, so universal is this second century reverence for the authoritative teaching office of the apostles that the saying of Serapion, Bishop of Antioch about AD 180, 'We accept the apostles as the Lord Himself' could with no less truth have been written eighty years earlier.

We have seen, then, that the traditional attitude of the Christian Church to the Scriptures as the supreme judge both of doctrine and life springs from the attitude of Jesus Himself to the Scriptures of the Old Testament. We have seen reason to believe that He intended the same to apply to the Scriptures of the New Testament, and that not only did the apostles unambiguously claim this authority, but the early church endorsed their claim. If we are to follow their example, and make the Bible the final authority under God for our Christian lives, what intellectual and practical consequences will follow?

Intellectual consequences of the Traditional view

1. In the first place, it should hardly need saying that *we are not confined to any particular theory of inspiration.* Because we hold to the supreme authority of the Bible, we need not suppose that there was anything mechanical in

God's inspiration of the sacred writers, as if they were God's secretaries to whom He dictated His letters! They were, of course, creatures of their age; they wrote for an immediate situation; some of them were kings and politicians, some were shepherds and fishermen. Some wrote polished poetry or limpid prose; others were scarcely grammatical. The point is that God brought about the varied circumstances of the particular age in which He put them, and then revealed to them His purpose in and through those circumstances, without doing any violence to the human individuality of the Biblical authors.

How we would love to understand how this dual authorship worked! How was it that God overruled all that was written by the human authors, so that nothing was omitted that He wished to be there, and nothing included which was against His will? The Bible never explains this to us. The nearest we get to an answer is 2 Peter 1.21, where we are told that holy men of God (i.e., men who had deliberately set themselves apart for God's service) were carried along by the Holy Spirit. The metaphor hinted at, in the Greek words used, is perhaps significant. It suggests that, just as sailors hoist the sail and wait for the wind to fill it and carry them along, so the sacred writers put themselves at the disposal of the Holy Spirit for Him to come and fill them, and carry them along in the direction of His choice. But this is merely a guess. Wisely the Church has never pronounced on the *mode* of inspiration, but has been jealous to safeguard the *fact* of it. The actual psychology of inspiration is not discussed in the Bible or the early church. The biblical writers affirm that the Scriptures are inspired by God. They do not attempt to explain how, and neither should we.

2. In the second place, *we are not reduced to a false literalism.* This is a common ground of complaint against the traditional position, but it is as much beside the point as the previous one. It is no part of the Christian faith to regard as statements of fact what is obviously poetic imagery. The Bible is a very varied book, and employs poetry, song, history, teaching, parable, proverb, allegory and other literary forms as vehicles for its message. The task of the Bible student is to try to discover what type of

literature is being presented at any given point, and apply to it the criteria proper to that type of literature, so as to understand its meaning. For example, the central issue in Genesis 1-3 is one of authority not of interpretation. Our *interpretation* will differ according to whether we regard it as straightforward history or as a poetic story, couched in non-scientific language and designed to teach abiding spiritual truth. But we bow to the *authority* of its message if we stay true to the revelation it contains—the sovereignty of God, His creative activity, the creation of man, his original goodness and fall into sin, resulting in his penal separation from the enjoyment of the presence of God. This is the teaching of the passage, and it is clearly quite a different matter from the literary *genre* employed.

We do God no honour by applying to poetry like Job the canons proper to prose like the Acts. A statement can perfectly well be true without being literal. Psalm 18.8ff gives a brilliant picture of God's majesty, but I do not think we are to imagine that smoke *literally* went up from His nostrils, or fire from His mouth, or that He rode upon a cherub!

We are told in Revelation 21.21 that the streets of the heavenly City are pure gold. It would be impossible for God to tell us exactly what heaven was like; He has to do it in picture language, just as we try to explain to a child something he has never experienced in terms of what he *does* understand. Such descriptions are not meant to be taken literally, but to excite our wonder and longing for the reality of which they give a faint glimmer. We may be quite sure that the picture of the new Jerusalem, dazzling though it is, falls very far short of the reality.

Or take the story of Jonah. It *may* be meant as straightforward history, particularly as we know of a Jonah from 2 Kings 14.25, and as Jesus referred to his sojourn in the belly of the great fish (e.g., Matthew 12.40). On the other hand, we may be meant to read it as a parable to teach us the importance of missionary work. Admittedly, it does not say that it is a parable. But then, neither does the story of the Prodigal Son! And I do not suppose that anybody feels that the importance of the teaching of that story depends on whether there was such a son or not.

The important thing is not whether we regard the stories of Jonah and the Prodigal as historical or parabolical (on that there may be legitimate differences of opinion) but on whether we bow to the divine authoritativeness of the message they enshrine.

Literalism, then, is no essential part of any orthodox doctrine of Scripture.

3. Thirdly, *we are not compelled to assign an equal value to all parts of the Bible* once we assert that they are all inspired by God. Of course the genealogies in Numbers are not of the same *value* to us as the Fourth Gospel! But they may both be equally inspired, that is to say, the product of the divine will. They may both equally serve His purpose, though it goes without saying that St John's Gospel has a far more important place in God's plan. The hairs on our head and our eyes are both nourished by the same blood stream. But it goes without saying that our eyes are of greater value to us than our hair!

4. Fourthly, *we are not to suppose that everything in the Bible commands our belief and obedience* irrespective of the speaker, or the context. It does not. It is the *doctrine* of the Bible that we are to believe and obey. The advice of Job's comforters and the statement of the fool that there is no God, are no part of the doctrine of the Bible and we are not bound to believe them! Abraham's duplicity in passing off his wife as his sister, Solomon's polygamy, or the fierce language of some of the imprecatory psalms are not recorded for our emulation. To suppose that they are is to imagine that God will never teach us by warnings, or discourage us from evil by showing us its result in the shipwreck of some disobedient man's life. Quite apart from this, the Bible is the record of a God who rescues sinners. It never hides or excuses the failures of its heroes.

Some parts of the Bible have reference only to a particular place and time; for example we do not today refrain from eating meat that has been strangled, as the early Gentile Christians were bound to do if they were to eat at the table with their Jewish Christian brethren (Acts 15.29). But if we are wise, we will follow the principle behind this regulation—and be prepared to agree to some personal inconvenience and flexibility of behaviour in order to show our fellowship with other Christians who may differ from us in customs or worship. The principle holds good, even though the situation to which it applied in the Bible has long since disappeared.

Again, in 1 Corinthians 11, St Paul argues at great length that women should not appear in church at Corinth unveiled. Today we do not think a woman immodest if she comes to church without a hat on. Social customs have changed, and St Paul's actual command is no longer appropriate; but the principle behind it is. A Christian woman in 20th century England should avoid any suggestion of indecency just as carefully as her Corinthian sister did.

In other words, it is impossible to treat the Bible like an Old Moore's Almanac, and suppose that one can go straight from its pages to action irrespective of the context and of the original situation addressed. We must distinguish between the Bible itself and the teaching of the Bible. It is the latter which is the Word of God that we must obey. And it is interesting to note that in the New Testament it is the biblical message as a whole and not the books of the Bible that are called the Word of God (e.g., 1 Thessalonians 2.13). Thus, if I am persuaded that a doctrine is biblical, I will both accept it and teach it. I will not consider myself at liberty to reject it if I do not happen to like it, or do not understand how it can be so. Universalism is a case in point. I would like nothing better than to believe that there is no hell, and that all men will be saved. But universalism was never deduced from the pages of Scripture. It is the product of the human mind which cannot reconcile the eternal loss of any man with the love of God. Neither can I, but if I desert the plain teaching of the whole Bible, and in particular of Jesus Christ, on this dread subject of hell, and teach universalism, then I am bowing to the supremacy of Reason over Scripture, and am deserting the orthodox attitude to the Bible for what we have called the 'Liberal' answer to the problem of authority.

Once this point is clearly appreciated, we are delivered from the paralysing fear that if one single discrepancy should be found in Scripture we should have to abandon all belief in its authority. The inerrancy of all minutiæ in the Bible account has never been the main concern of upholders of the supreme authority of the Scriptures. Some, like B. B. Warfield in *Inspiration and Authority of the Bible* have believed it; others, like J. Orr in *Revelation and Inspiration*, have not, but have thought that small discrepancies, such as those in the gospel accounts of the resurrection, actually strengthen the case for the reliability of the Biblical authors, and show that they were in no sort of collusion as to the facts they relate. As Chrysostom put it, 'The very fact of discrepancies is a very great evidence of the truth of the evangelists. For if they had agreed in all things exactly even to time, and place, and to the very words, none of our enemies would have believed but that they had met together, and had written what they wrote by some human compact. . . . But now even that discordance which seems to exist in little matters delivers them from all suspicion, and speaks clearly in behalf of the character of the writers' (*Homily on Matthew* 1.6). Whether or not it may be possible to harmonize all apparent discrepancies, or to solve all difficulties in the Biblical accounts, is beside the point. There is, as Chrysostom goes on to maintain, no difference whatever among the New Testament writers in 'the chief heads of their doctrine, wherein nowhere are they found to disagree, no not ever so little'. He instances such doctrines as, 'that God became man, that He wrought miracles, that He was crucified, that He rose again, that He ascended, that He will judge'.

Not that the Bible is full of discrepancies. Very far from it. Every fresh archæological discovery tends to show how trustworthy the inspired record is. Indeed, there is not, so far as I know, a single discrepancy that it is quite impossible to reconcile. But there are many *apparent* discrepancies, which seem at first sight to be unanswerable. Our attitude to these should be to study them carefully, and be prepared to withhold judgment for the time being until we are better able to judge. For example, for years it used to be thought that St John's statement that Pilate tried Jesus 'at a place called the Pavement, and in Hebrew, Gabbatha' (19.13) was quite unhistorical—a bit of late embroidery on the simple story of the crucifixion! The scholars knew very well that there never was such a pavement. But a few years ago it was discovered some fifteen feet below the surface of present day Jerusalem. It measured some fifty yards in each direction, and was the courtyard of the Roman barracks in Jerusalem. The same was said about the pool of Bethesda with its five porches (John 5). This, too, was regarded as mythical, since not only had no trace of it been discovered, but there was no reference to it anywhere in ancient literature outside St John. But now, not only have the porticoes of Bethesda been dug up, but the name has occurred in one of the scrolls at Qumran!

To take another example, a comparatively short while ago it was said that the Acts of the Apostles was unreliable in making Gallio proconsul of Achaea (Acts 18). We happen to know a good deal about Gallio, because he was the brother of the famous Seneca, and his career could be so well reconstructed that there scarcely seemed any possibility of his having been proconsul of Achaea. The outlook for St Luke's reliability seemed very bleak indeed —until an inscription turned up in Delphi (of all unlikely places) which not only showed that Gallio *was* proconsul of Achaea, but gives us the date when he was so! And now what used to be thought an error in St Luke has turned out to be the lynch-pin of New Testament chronology! All of which should warn us against jumping to hasty conclusions when faced with a difficulty in the Bible.

At all events, orthodox Christians down the ages have reverenced the Bible as the inspired record of God's self-revelation to men, containing the truth about God and man, about heaven and hell, and supremely about Jesus Christ and the salvation He offers to all. Not only have they reverenced it, but they have refused to believe that Church tradition should alter, or human reason deny, what God has been pleased to reveal of Himself in the Scriptures. Scripture, in short, is to be the norm, the standard in all matters of faith and conduct. It is to this that we are committed if we are to be true, not only to the example of our Master, but to the clearly defined teaching of the Church of England.

If these are some of the intellectual consequences that would seem to follow from the attitude of our Saviour to His Bible, what of the practical consequences?

Practical consequences of the Traditional view

1. In the first place, *we should come humbly to the study of the Bible.* We must never forget that the 'natural man' can neither receive nor understand the things of the Spirit of God (1 Corinthians 2.14). They are hid from the wise and prudent, and revealed to babes (Matthew 11.25). It is possible, as the Reformation made plain, for the simple, diligent Bible student who really knows his Lord, to have a firmer grasp of the doctrines of the Bible, a clearer understanding *in practice* of the will of God and His salvation, than some brilliant professor who has never come as a sinner to be forgiven, and has never submitted his will to the divine will. We ought to come to Scripture not to judge it, but to be judged by it. We shall not concern ourselves exclusively with 'problems', but seek for spiritual nourishment. When difficulties arise, we shall look for harmony, we shall pray for understanding. We shall not be so foolish as to suppose that if we cannot see the answer to some difficulty, no answer exists! We shall, no doubt, refer to a modern translation; we shall examine the context again; we may well go away to ask some more experienced Christian or to look in a commentary. If we are wise, we shall compare the passage with some other part of Scripture and see if that will bring any light on the problem. Above all we shall lay our difficulty before God in prayer, coming to Him in a humble, teachable attitude. For God cannot teach a proud man. Indeed, He resists the proud, but gives His help to the humble (1 Peter 5.5).

2. Secondly, *we shall seek Christ in the Bible.* There is no small danger these days of regarding the Scriptures

primarily as an object of belief, rather than as a means of contact with Christ. It is interesting that in the historic creeds of Christendom the authority and inspiration of the Bible is never made an explicit article of faith—and yet it is constantly assumed. The old creedmakers were perfectly right. In the jargon of today we would say that they recognized the 'existential' significance of the Bible. The Scriptures, that is to say, are a message from a personal God to living people in a real situation, and we must never de-personalize the Word of God, and, like the Jews of old, make it an object of veneration distinct from the God who gave it. The Bible is meant to lead us to what Buber has called an 'I-Thou' relationship with God. We must never allow this to degenerate into an 'I-It' relationship, with the Bible as the object of our attention. To quote Martin Luther, 'As we go to the cradle only in order to find the baby, so we go to the Scriptures only to find Christ'. There are, in all the Scriptures, things concerning Himself (Luke 24.27). It is interesting that the phrase 'the Word of God' is applied in the Bible both to the Scriptures and to Christ. It is in the written Word that we find the living Word, who alone is the food for our souls. The Scriptures testify of Him, and only in coming to Him can we have life (John 5.39, 40). It is tragically possible to be a diligent student of the Bible, and yet to become quite deaf to the voice of Christ to us in its pages. We shall avoid that danger if, each time we come to read, we ask the Lord to speak to us personally through some word, some verse, some thought in the passage we are about to read. A determination to seek Christ in our reading of Scripture will save us from a barren orthodoxy.

3. Thirdly, *we shall need to study the Bible.* The Christian who regards it as his greatest authority under God for the things he believes and the way he lives his life, cannot afford to treat it superficially. If this Book can show us more of God's will for our lives, if it can bring us face to face with our ascended Master, then it is the most important thing we can study. '*Study,*' says Paul to Timothy, 'Study to show thyself approved unto God, a workman that needeth not to be ashamed, rightly dividing

(*literally*, "driving a straight furrow through") the word of truth' (2 Timothy 2.15, AV). This will mean making time in our busy lives. We shall need the help of a concordance, and of good commentaries. The man who takes his Bible study seriously will not suppose that an isolated text will always give him the *whole* biblical view on any subject; and he will want, from time to time, to study a subject, a Bible character, a significant word, perhaps a whole book, with at least as much care as he would give to his daily work.

4. Having studied the Bible, *we shall be able to apply it* to our circumstances and needs. Two of the questions we should continually be asking of any portion of the Bible are first, 'What did this mean to the original people concerned?' In this way we shall ensure that we are not ripping it from its context or otherwise misinterpreting it. And secondly we must ask, 'What does this mean to *me?*' In this way we shall ensure that we are making what we read relevant to our lives. After all, this is the purpose for which God gave us the Bible. He did not intend it to be a text book of mystical doctrines, but a guide to the sort of life that is pleasing to Him. It does not contain all we should *like* to know, but it does contain all we *need* to know in order to enjoy a right relationship with God and live a holy and effective Christian life.

5. Fifthly, *we shall need to take care to obey* the Bible. It is all too easy to be a hearer of the Word and not a doer (James 1.22). This danger increases as our familiarity with the Bible and its commands grows. It is a temptation to which Christian leaders and clergy are particularly prone. It is, therefore, most important to remember that God gives us indications of His will in order that we may follow them, and if we do not, we are guilty of disobeying God. As Peter reminded the high priest, the Holy Spirit is given by God to them that *obey* Him (Acts 5.32). It was because the Jewish leaders resisted the Holy Spirit (Acts 7.51) and were disobedient to the will of God as revealed in the Scriptures, that their minds were blinded, and, as it were, a veil was over their eyes as they read the Old Testament (2 Corinthians 3.14). That is a warning of

what can happen to any man, if he does not obey what he knows to be God's will.

6. Finally, *let us use the Bible*, as we seek to be of help to those within the Christian Church, and as we reach forth to those outside it. It is very significant that St Paul committed his Ephesian friends, whom he thought he would never see again, 'to God and to the word of his grace, which is able to build you up and to give you the inheritance among all those who are sanctified' (Acts 20.32). Now it is natural enough to commit a Christian friend to God, when you have to be parted from him. But the fact that in this greeting Paul couples *God's gracious message* together with God Himself shows how tremendously highly he valued the Scriptures, and how much store he set by their use. For the Scriptures will build the Christian up, and they will show him more and more of his inheritance in Christ.

Again, on the day of Pentecost men were pricked in their heart when they heard Peter preaching the message of God's Saviour, His cross and resurrection, and His claims on their obedience. And people are still pricked in the heart when confronted by the message of the gospel. It is still the power of God for salvation to every one who believes (Romans 1.16). If we believe in the authority of the Bible, we shall make every effort to pass on its message to those who are in ignorance of it. Indeed, the New Testament records show us example after example of amateur missionaries using the Scriptures (of the Old Testament—because, as yet, there was no New Testament) to bring home to their audience the message of the gospel. Very often that audience must have been just one man, as when Philip spoke to the Ethiopian official in his chariot. But here the same principle of using the Bible held good; he showed him the gospel out of the Scriptures, in this case Isaiah 53 (Acts 8.32-35).

Here, surely, is a pointer for us. Any Christian can speak to individual friends about the message of the Gospel. He will discover that time and again the divine authority of the Word of God is borne out in experience. He will come to believe it, not simply because Jesus did, nor because the early church did, nor because the formularies of our Church do, but because it works in practice.

Of course there will be disappointments and difficulties. But to have begun to use the Scriptures for the very purposes for which they were intended, will bring the joy of seeing others respond to the love of Christ which has gripped us, and will leave very little room for further doubts about the divine inspiration and authority of Holy Scripture.